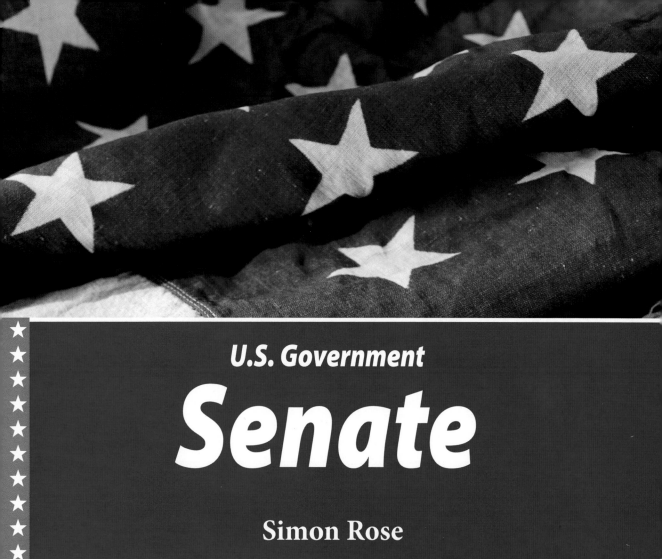

U.S. Government

Senate

Simon Rose

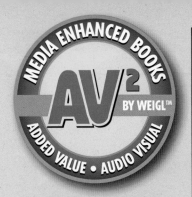

AV² provides enriched content that supplements and complements this book. Weigl's AV² books strive to create inspired learning and engage young minds in a total learning experience.

Your AV² Media Enhanced books come alive with...

 Audio
Listen to sections of the book read aloud.

 Key Words
Study vocabulary, and complete a matching word activity.

 Video
Watch informative video clips.

 Quizzes
Test your knowledge.

Go to **www.av2books.com**, and enter this book's unique code.

 Embedded Weblinks
Gain additional information for research.

 Slide Show
View images and captions, and prepare a presentation.

BOOK CODE

P304648

AV² by Weigl brings you media enhanced books that support active learning.

 Try This!
Complete activities and hands-on experiments.

... and much, much more!

Published by AV² by Weigl
350 5th Avenue, 59th Floor
New York, NY 10118

Websites: www.av2books.com   www.weigl.com

Library of Congress Cataloging-in-Publication Data

Rose, Simon, 1961-
Senate / Simon Rose.
     pages cm. — (U.S. government)
Includes bibliographical references and index.
ISBN 978-1-4896-1942-6 (hardcover: alk. paper) — ISBN 978-1-4896-1943-3 (softcover: alk. paper) —
ISBN 978-1-4896-1944-0 (single user ebook) — ISBN 978-1-4896-1945-7 (multi user ebook)
1. United States. Congress. Senate—Juvenile literature. 2. Legislators--United States—Juvenile literature.
3. Legislation—United States—Juvenile literature. I. Title.
JK1276.R67 2015
328.73'071—dc23
                    2014009520

Printed in the United States of America in North Mankato, Minnesota
1 2 3 4 5 6 7 8 9 0 18 17 16 15 14

062014
WEP270514

Senior Editor: Heather Kissock
Art Director: Terry Paulhus

Weigl acknowledges Getty Images as its primary image supplier for this title.

Contents

The Government of the United States

If the United States had no government, there would be no armed forces to protect the country. There would be no laws to keep air and water clean, and there would be no system to manage air traffic at airports. Many aspects of people's lives are affected by government decisions, past and present.

The United States is a democracy, which means its leaders are elected by the people. The national government has three branches. The executive branch carries out laws. It includes the president, the **vice president**, the **cabinet** departments, and government agencies. The legislative branch, which passes laws, is made up of Congress. This branch has two chambers, or parts. They are the Senate and the House of Representatives. The judicial branch, which enforces laws, includes the Supreme Court. This is the highest-level legal body in the United States. The judicial branch also includes several other types of courts.

The three branches of government balance each other. For example, although Congress creates laws, the president has the power to **veto** them. The Supreme Court can decide that laws do not agree with the U.S. **Constitution**. The president is elected, but in special cases, Congress has the power to remove a president from office. The president **nominates** judges to the Supreme Court, but the Senate must approve them.

Washington, D.C.

The main center of the U.S. government is in the country's capital, Washington, D.C.

White House

The president lives and works in the White House. Part of the president's staff works there, too.

Capitol Building

The Senate and the House of Representatives meet in the U.S. Capitol.

Supreme Court Building

The Supreme Court decides cases affecting the nation in the Supreme Court Building.

Work on the Capitol Building began in 1793. Since then, it has been rebuilt, expanded, and restored.

The Federal System

FOCUS

★ *National, state, and local governments share power*
★ *Each level of government has different areas of responsibility*
★ *The U.S. government deals with issues affecting the whole country*
★ *State and local governments have the main responsibility for schools, parks, and public transportation*

The United States has a federal system of government. This means that power is shared between the national, state, and local governments. The national government is also known as the federal government.

The three levels of government have different powers and responsibilities. Each of the 50 states has its own constitution, and the responsibilities of the federal and state governments are usually clearly defined. However, sometimes disputes occur that have to be settled by the Supreme Court.

The federal government deals with issues affecting the whole country. These include defending the nation, issuing money, and regulating the country's **economy**. The federal government also manages U.S. relations with other nations.

The states have the main responsibility for stopping crime, setting up local governments, and regulating businesses within the state. Some responsibilities exist at both the federal and state levels. These include **taxation**, setting up courts, and building highways.

State governments are generally responsible for education in their area.

There are several types of local governments, including cities, towns, and counties. Counties are known as parishes in Louisiana and boroughs in Alaska. Local governments are responsible for police, fire, and emergency medical services. They also manage parks, public transportation, trash collection, and sewer systems.

The Federal Government

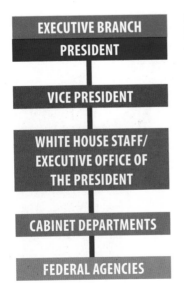

EXECUTIVE BRANCH	LEGISLATIVE BRANCH	JUDICIAL BRANCH
PRESIDENT	CONGRESS	SUPREME COURT
VICE PRESIDENT		COURTS OF APPEALS
WHITE HOUSE STAFF/ EXECUTIVE OFFICE OF THE PRESIDENT	SENATE HOUSE OF REPRESENTATIVES	DISTRICT COURTS
CABINET DEPARTMENTS		SPECIAL COURTS
FEDERAL AGENCIES		

The Senate

FOCUS

★ *The Senate has 100 members, two from each state*

★ *The Senate and the House of Representatives serve as a check on each other*

★ *Senators are elected by voters in their state*

★ *The vice president of the United States can oversee meetings of the Senate*

The Senate has 100 senators, two from each of the 50 states. Although the states have different populations, each state is equally represented in the Senate. This gives more power there to small states. The Senate has fewer members than the House of Representatives. In the House, the number of members from each state is based on the state's population. This gives more power there to the larger states. In this way, the two chambers serve as a check on each other.

At first, senators were chosen by state legislatures. In 1913, this system was changed by the 17th **Amendment**. It let people in each state vote for their senators.

Richard Durbin of Illinois was elected to the Senate in 1996. He has held Democratic Party leadership positions since 2005.

In January 2014, senators joined members of the House of Representatives to hear a speech by President Barack Obama. He urged Congress to pass new laws that he favored.

The vice president of the United States can **preside** over meetings of the Senate. However, this happens rarely. The vice president can vote in the Senate only to break a tie. If a close vote is expected, the vice president may attend a Senate meeting to cast the tie-breaking vote if necessary.

The two major **political parties** both have leaders in the Senate. The leader of the party with the most senators is called the majority leader. The leader of the other party is called the minority leader.

History of the Senate

In 1787, the U.S. Constitution established a legislature with two branches. Congress met for the first time in New York City in 1789. From 1790 to 1800, Congress met in Philadelphia, Pennsylvania. In 1800, Washington, D.C., became the nation's capital, and Congress moved into the Capitol Building.

There were 26 senators in the first Congress. At the time, there were only 13 states. When a new state is created, two new members are added to the Senate. The total number of senators has been 100 since Alaska and Hawai'i became states in 1959.

The Senate has been the site of many important discussions and decisions. In 1820, for example, after **debates** in the chamber, the Senate agreed to the Missouri Compromise. This was an attempt to regulate slavery in new western territories and keep power equal between the northern and southern states in the federal government. However, in the end, no lasting agreement could be reached on slavery, and the Civil War took place.

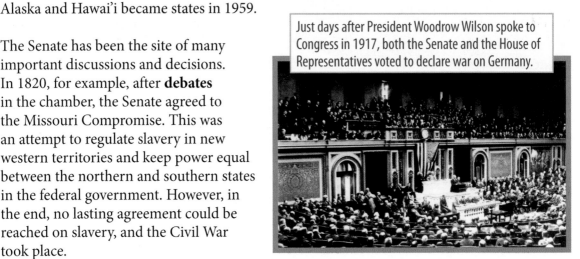

Just days after President Woodrow Wilson spoke to Congress in 1917, both the Senate and the House of Representatives voted to declare war on Germany.

President Woodrow Wilson addressed both chambers of Congress in 1917 to ask for a declaration of war in World War I. The Constitution makes the president the commander in chief of the U.S. armed forces, but it gives Congress the power to declare war. The Senate and the House of Representatives issued an official declaration of war.

In 2001, Hillary Rodham Clinton, President Bill Clinton's wife, became the first former First Lady to serve in the Senate.

In 1941, the Senate and the House also issued a declaration of war for the United States to enter World War II. At the end of that war, President Harry Truman spoke to the Senate about ratifying, or approving, the **United Nations** (UN) Charter. The Senate approved, and the United States became a founding member of the UN.

The Senate has held presidential **impeachment** trials twice. The most recent was in 1999, when President Bill Clinton was tried. He was acquitted, or found not guilty.

CHANGES OVER TIME

1814 – The Capitol is seriously damaged by British troops in the War of 1812.

1816 – The Senate establishes the system of standing, or permanent, **committees**.

1975 – Senate committee meetings are first opened to the public.

1986 – Regular television coverage of Senate meetings begins.

1995 – The Senate launches its first home page on the internet.

Role of the Senate

FOCUS

★ *Members of the Senate introduce and pass bills to make new laws*

★ *The Senate acts as the jury during impeachment trials*

★ *The Senate must approve treaties the president makes with other countries*

★ *The Senate must approve many presidential appointments*

★ *The Senate carries out investigations*

The U.S. Constitution describes the powers of the two chambers of Congress. The Senate and the House of Representatives share many powers. The Senate, however, has some specific roles.

Creating laws is the most important job of Congress. Another name for laws is legislation. The process of making laws is also sometimes called legislation. Long debates in the Senate and the House make sure that all aspects of legislation are fully discussed. For an **act** of Congress to become law, both the Senate and the House must approve it.

Debates about legislation in the Senate can, in theory, go on forever. Senators can **filibuster** to delay or block a vote. A process called cloture is the only way to end a filibuster. This needs a vote by three-fifths of the membership, or 60 senators.

Members of each political party often speak to reporters to discuss how their party feels about important issues.

The House of Representatives can impeach federal officials because of wrongdoing. The Senate conducts the trial and acts as the jury. A two-thirds vote in the Senate is needed to remove an official from office.

The president negotiates treaties, or agreements, with other countries, but the Senate has to ratify them. Senators must also approve major presidential appointments, such as members of the cabinet, Supreme Court justices, and U.S. ambassadors to other countries. The Senate also carries out investigations. It has investigated organized crime, the Vietnam War, and the Watergate scandal, which involved illegal actions by White House officials. The Watergate investigation led to the resignation of President Richard Nixon in 1974.

SENATE COMMITTEES

Before bills, or proposed laws, are presented in the entire Senate, they are sent to committees. These are groups of senators set up to study particular areas. They include agriculture, the armed forces, education, energy and natural resources, foreign relations, transportation, and veterans' affairs. A bill is sent to the committee handling its topic. For example, a bill to provide aid to farmers during a drought would go to the agriculture committee.

How a Bill Is Passed

Congress considers many bills during each session, the period of time during which Congress meets regularly. Only a small number are passed and then signed into law by the president. Bills on most subjects may be introduced in either part of Congress. Each bill goes through a long legislative process. This includes committee meetings, debates, and possible amendments in both the Senate and the House of Representatives.

1 Introduction in the Senate

A member of the Senate introduces a bill. If there are no objections to it, it is read twice, printed, and given a number. The senator who introduced it is known as the bill's sponsor.

2 Consideration by Committee

The bill is sent to a Senate committee. Committee members study every detail of the bill. Then, they vote on the bill. If a majority of committee members approves it, a report on the bill is written.

3 Debate by Senators

The bill is then placed on the Senate's calendar and is debated by all of the senators. They discuss the bill and may suggest amendments. These are debated and voted on separately.

Many people attend committee hearings when an important bill is being considered.

During committee meetings, members may meet with experts and government officials. They want to better understand how a bill might affect the nation. Public hearings may also take place, at which people express their views about the bill.

4 The Senate Votes

At the end of the debate, and when any proposed amendments have been approved, the Senate votes on the bill. If it passes, the bill is sent to the House of Representatives.

5 Action in the House

The House may approve, reject, or amend the bill. If there are amendments, a joint Senate and House committee meets to discuss the bill's two versions. When agreement is reached on a compromise bill, each chamber then votes again on the final version.

6 Action by the President

If both chambers vote to pass the bill, it is sent to the president. He or she can sign the bill into law. If the president disagrees with the bill, he or she can veto it. Congress can override a presidential veto. This requires a two-thirds majority vote of all members present in both the Senate and the House.

Thomas Ustick Walter, who served as architect of the Capitol in the mid-1800s, designed the room, also called the chamber, where the U.S. Senate meets today. The Senate's proceedings, or meetings, have been held there since January 1859. The chamber was renovated from 1949 to 1950 to improve the lighting, air circulation, and sound quality. The Old Senate Chamber, where the Senate met from 1819 to 1859, is also in the Capitol Building. It is now a museum and is sometimes used for ceremonies or special meetings.

The Senate Chamber

The Senate chamber is a rectangular room that is two stories high. It is located in the north wing of the Capitol, on the second floor. The room has no windows. The ceiling is made of stainless steel and plaster.

1 Senators' Desks

The Senate chamber has 100 desks, one for each senator. The desks are divided according to the political parties of the members, with Democrats on one side of the room and Republicans on the other side. The desks are arranged in a semicircle. They face the central dais, or platform. Senators usually choose a desk based on their **seniority** in their party. Many senators sign their name in the drawer of their desk.

2 The Central Dais

The central dais is where the presiding officer of the Senate sits while he or she is managing the Senate's proceedings. Four people sit at desks below the presiding officer. They are the assistant secretary, the legislative clerk, the parliamentarian, who advises on rules and procedures, and the journal clerk. The journal is a record of the Senate's proceedings.

4 The Gallery

The Senate gallery is located above the main floor, on all four sides of the room. When the Senate is in session, visitors can watch the proceedings from the gallery. Passes are required to enter the gallery. Visitors can obtain passes from their senators' offices. Visitors also can take tours of the rest of the Capitol Building.

3 Press Gallery

Reporters who cover the Senate's proceedings sit in the press gallery. This is a section of the regular gallery. People using the press gallery include newspaper reporters, television journalists, and reporters for internet sites. Reporters often interview senators directly in the halls of the Capitol.

Key Positions

A number of positions in the Senate are important in making sure that it operates effectively. The leaders of the political parties organize their members. The Senate also has officers who advise senators on the rules of the chamber. Among these officers are the secretary of the Senate, the parliamentarian, and the sergeant at arms, who enforces the rules.

Presiding Officers

The U.S. vice president also has the title president of the Senate. When the vice president is not present, the president pro tempore oversees the Senate. The members of the Senate elect the president pro tempore. He or she is usually the member of the party with the most seats in the Senate who has served the longest.

Majority Leader

Members of the party with the most seats in the Senate elect the Senate majority leader. This person acts as the party's spokesperson on important issues and represents the party in the chamber. The majority leader is also a spokesperson for the whole Senate and manages the chamber's schedule.

Before becoming vice president, Joe Biden was a senator from Delaware from 1973 to 2009.

In 2007, Harry Reid of Nevada became the Senate majority leader.

Minority Leader Members of the party with fewer seats in the Senate elect the Senate minority leader. This person represents his or her party in the chamber. He or she is also the spokesperson for the party's official position on the different bills presented in the Senate.

Whips Both political parties have whips. The whips manage the votes of party members. They make sure these senators are ready to vote on bills and know how party leaders want them to vote. The whips also make sure that the members are up to date on all current business in the chamber.

BECOMING A SENATOR

A senator must be at least 30 years old and a resident of the state he or she represents. In addition, a senator must have been a U.S. **citizen** for at least nine years. Senators are elected to serve for six years, and one-third of the Senate is elected every two years. Sometimes, senators have to be replaced. For example, a senator might die while serving in office or resign to accept another position. In most cases, the governor of the state that the senator is from names a replacement. Sometimes, a special election is held to choose a replacement.

In the months before Election Day, Senate candidates spend a great deal of time meeting residents of their state, hoping to win their support.

A Day in the Life

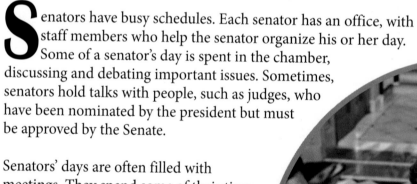

FOCUS

★ *Senators discuss and debate issues on the Senate floor*

★ *They spend much of their time in committee meetings*

★ *They meet with the people they represent and other groups*

★ *They spend time in their home state and also travel internationally*

Senators have busy schedules. Each senator has an office, with staff members who help the senator organize his or her day. Some of a senator's day is spent in the chamber, discussing and debating important issues. Sometimes, senators hold talks with people, such as judges, who have been nominated by the president but must be approved by the Senate.

Senators' days are often filled with meetings. They spend some of their time with members of the committees they belong to, studying the details of bills. Each senator is a member of a number of different Senate committees. A senator may also be a member of a joint committee. These are made up of both senators and representatives.

Dianne Feinstein of California, who has served in the Senate since 1992, is a member of the committee that considers Supreme Court appointments.

Senators also gather to discuss issues raised in debates or to receive updates on the work of other committees. Each political party's Senate leaders schedule conferences to plan for debates. Senators get together as well with the people they represent or with **lobbyists** and **interest groups**. They may hear from groups who are concerned about child welfare, the care of the elderly, and other issues. Then, they are able to raise these concerns on the Senate floor.

Ted Cruz of Texas defeated several other candidates to win election to the Senate in 2012.

On some days, senators have discussions with people representing industries, labor unions, and volunteer organizations. Senators often are questioned by reporters from newspapers and television stations. Their day is not over when they leave the Senate. Senators often attend events in the evenings, such as fundraisers to collect money for worthy causes or for their next election **campaign**.

TRAVELING

Senators spend a great deal of time in Washington when the Senate is in session and bills are being presented. At other times, they travel, often to attend conferences and other meetings. Some senators travel to other countries on behalf of the United States. They get together with officials from these nations to discuss issues such as human rights, trade, and security. Senators also spend time in their home states, where they maintain offices. They try to understand the interests and needs of the citizens of their states, so that they can represent them well.

★ Important Moments

T he Senate has played a role in some of the most important decisions made by the U.S. government. It almost removed a president from office. In addition, some of the most notable speeches in American history have taken place on the Senate floor.

Daniel Webster's Speech on Slavery 1850

On March 7, 1850, Massachusetts Senator Daniel Webster gave a speech in the Senate in support of a proposal called the Compromise of 1850. The issue was slavery. Webster spoke for more than three hours. He urged northerners to respect slavery, which existed mostly in the southern states. He said that people who owned slaves had a right to their property and that laws about the capture of runaway slaves should be made stronger. Some people praised Webster for his courage, but northerners who were opposed to slavery were very angry. Webster's political career was ruined, and he soon resigned from the Senate.

Impeachment Trial of Andrew Johnson 1868

Andrew Johnson became president following the assassination, or killing, of Abraham Lincoln in 1865. There were disagreements between Johnson and Congress after the Civil War. Johnson vetoed many of the bills sent to him. Many members of Congress felt that he was not acting properly as president. They wanted to remove him from office. After the House impeached Johnson, his trial took place in the Senate. The final vote to convict him was 35 to 19. This was one vote short of the two-thirds majority needed to remove Johnson from office.

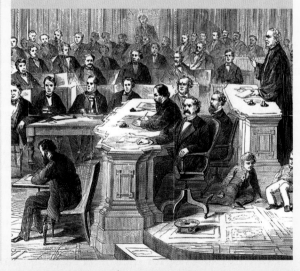

The Treaty of Versailles 1919

President Woodrow Wilson played a major role in writing the Treaty of Versailles, which ended World War I. It also helped to create the League of Nations, an organization that was designed to keep the peace in the future. The treaty had to be approved by the Senate. Wilson delivered the treaty to the chamber himself in July 1919. He made a speech, asking the Senate to approve the treaty. Some senators were angry because they had not taken part in the talks to arrive at the treaty. Others felt that joining the League of Nations would involve the United States in foreign disputes that might lead to war. Some senators wanted to change the treaty. Wilson refused to compromise, and the Senate rejected the treaty. It was the first time the Senate had rejected a peace treaty.

Winston Churchill's Address to Congress 1941

On December 26, 1941, Prime Minister Winston Churchill of Great Britain addressed a **joint session** of Congress in the Senate chamber. The United States had entered World War II less than three weeks earlier, following the Japanese attack on Pearl Harbor in Hawai'i. Churchill encouraged Congress to support President Franklin D. Roosevelt during the war. He warned that a great deal of hardship lay ahead before final victory could be certain. His speech strengthened the ties between the United States and Great Britain, which helped them to win the war.

The Civil Rights Act 1964

In February 1964, the House of Representatives approved a bill on civil rights. The bill would ban discrimination, or unfair treatment. It protected voting rights and established equal employment opportunities for all Americans, regardless of race. When the bill was introduced in the Senate, southern senators began a filibuster to block it. The chamber debated the bill for 60 days. On June 10, Senate leaders knew there were enough votes to end the filibuster. Senators voted for cloture and ended the debate. On June 19, the Senate passed the bill. President Lyndon Johnson signed the Civil Rights Act into law on July 2, 1964.

Significant Senators

Many men and women have served as senators since the Senate was first established. The earliest senators were men. The first woman was appointed to the Senate in 1922. She was Rebecca Latimer Felton of Georgia. The first African American was elected to the Senate in 1966. He was Edward Brooke of Massachusetts. Many senators have played leading roles in the history of the United States.

Robert La Follette (in office 1906–1925)

Robert La Follette (1855–1925) of Wisconsin served in the House of Representatives before becoming governor of his state. He served as governor from 1901 to 1906. As senator, La Follette worked for laws intended to help people rather than big business. These included rules for railroad companies and measures to help working children. He also supported allowing women to vote and promoting equal rights for all people. La Follette ran for president in 1924 but lost.

Arthur Vandenberg (in office 1928–1951)

Arthur Vandenberg (1884–1951) of Michigan opposed U.S. involvement in world affairs during the 1930s. However, when Japan attacked Pearl Harbor in December 1941, he decided that the United States had to enter World War II. After the war, Vandenberg was a strong supporter of the United Nations. He also was in favor of having the United States join NATO, an alliance with Great Britain and other countries. In addition, Vandenberg supported the Marshall Plan, a U.S. program to help Europe to rebuild after World War II.

Hattie Caraway (in office 1931–1944)

Hattie Caraway (1878–1950) of Arkansas was appointed to the Senate in November 1931 after her husband, who was serving as senator, died. Then, in January 1932, she won a special election and became the first woman to be elected to the Senate. In 1943, Caraway was the first woman to co-sponsor the Equal Rights Amendment. This proposal would have made equal rights for men and women a part of the U.S. Constitution. Caraway was also a strong supporter of the rights of federal workers who had been injured while working.

Robert Taft (in office 1939–1953)

Robert Taft (1889–1953) of Ohio was the Republican leader in the Senate for 14 years. He thought the government should not spend as much money as it did, and he believed that the federal government had too much power. Taft strongly opposed U.S. involvement in international affairs, but he supported U.S. efforts during World War II. After the war, Taft opposed joining international organizations such as NATO. He was the son of President William Howard Taft and wanted to become president himself. He ran for the Republican presidential nomination in 1948 and 1952, but he was unsuccessful.

Edward Kennedy (in office 1962–2009)

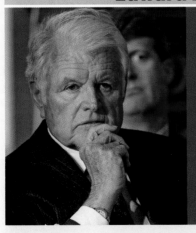

Edward Kennedy (1932–2009) of Massachusetts was the youngest brother of President John F. Kennedy and Senator Robert Kennedy. He was elected to the Senate when he was only 30. He was a strong supporter of civil rights, federal government spending on education, greater access to health care, and **immigration reform**. Kennedy, a member of the Democratic Party, worked with both Democrats and Republicans in the Senate and was the author of more than 2,000 bills. Hundreds of them became laws.

Issues Facing the Senate

FOCUS

- ★ **Senators may block or take a long time to approve appointments made by the president**
- ★ **If positions are not being filled promptly, the government may not function properly**
- ★ **The confirmation system is a check on the president's power**
- ★ **Senators need to raise millions of dollars for their campaigns, and the money may come from special interest groups**

Senators are responsible for confirming, or approving, many government appointments. Senators are supposed to consider nominations fairly, but this is not always the case. For political reasons, senators may reject people who are nominated by the president for certain jobs. They may also take a long time to give their approval. This may happen, for example, if the president is a Democrat and the Republican Party controls the Senate, or makes up the majority there. Then, Republican senators may decide to block presidential appointments. If this happens, positions are not filled promptly and the government may not work properly.

Despite problems, the confirmation system is important because it works as a check on the power of the president. Confirmations by the Senate make sure that the president is not giving jobs to friends and supporters. The system helps to make sure that well-qualified people are appointed. Senators are able to question nominees about their background and experience.

Hearings and a vote were held in the Senate after President Barack Obama nominated Elena Kagan to the Supreme Court in 2010.

Election campaigns for the Senate cost millions of dollars. As soon as a senator is elected, he or she needs to start raising money for the next campaign. This may mean the senator has less time for the job of making laws. A great deal of the money for campaigns comes from groups who want the senator to support their interests. The senator may want to keep the approval of these groups to make sure he or she is elected again. Some people believe that this affects senators' decisions in Congress. They think changes are needed to make sure that voters decide elections, not groups that give large amounts of money to a senator's campaign.

After they are elected, new members of the Senate are sworn in by the vice president.

However, others believe that giving money to campaigns is a way for people and organizations to make sure that their views are heard. Lobbyists work for special interest groups that give money to political campaigns. Some of the industries that lobbyists represent are oil and gas, insurance, and chemical companies. Lobbyists try to persuade senators to vote in a certain way on issues that affect their industries. If other groups or individuals give money to a senator's campaign, this helps to make sure that important issues are brought to the Senate's attention.

Activity

What is a debate?

When people debate a topic, two sides take a different viewpoint about one idea. They present logical arguments to support their views. Usually, each person or team is given a set amount of time to present its case. The presenters take turns stating their arguments until the total time set aside for the debate is used up. Sometimes, there is an audience in the room listening to the presentations. Later, the members of the audience vote for the person or team they think made the best arguments.

Debating is an important skill. It helps people to think about ideas carefully. It also helps them develop ways of speaking that others can follow easily. Some schools have debating clubs as part of their after-school activities. Debates are also often held in history classes. Students may debate when they are studying about world events.

Debate this!

Every day, the news is filled with the issues facing the United States and its citizens. These issues are debated by people and by those who represent them in Congress. People often have different views of these issues and support different solutions. Here is an issue that has been discussed across the country. Gather your friends or classmates, and divide into two teams to debate the issue. Each team should take time to research the issue and develop solid arguments for its side.

The U.S. Constitution does not say how long senators should serve. However, many Americans believe senators should have **term limits**. They think senators spend too much of their time working to get reelected. Also, they say, senators may become out of touch with the people in their state if they are in office too long.

Other people believe that regular elections already limit the number of terms senators serve. Senators will not be reelected if they have not served the people well. In addition, politicians who have done a good job should not be limited in the number of terms they serve. People should be allowed to vote for whomever they want.

 Should there be a limit on the number of terms a member of the Senate can serve?

★ Know Your Senate

1 Who was the first African American elected to the Senate?

2 How many members does the Senate have?

3 What is the minimum age to serve in the Senate?

4 What is the length of one Senate term?

5 When was the 17th Amendment to the U.S. Constitution passed?

6 What is the name for a long speech by a senator to delay or block a vote on a bill?

7 Who was the first former First Lady to serve in the Senate?

8 How are the desks divided in the Senate chamber?

9 Which senator ran unsuccessfully for the Republican presidential nomination in 1948 and 1952?

10 When did regular television coverage of Senate meetings begin?

Key Words

act: a bill that has been passed by both chambers of Congress and then has been signed by the president or has otherwise become law

amendment: a proposal to change the text of a bill or a document, such as the Constitution

cabinet: a group of people, many of them the heads of government departments, who give advice to the president

campaign: a series of activities to achieve a particular purpose, such as being elected to office

citizen: a person who is a legal resident of a country

committees: groups of people who discuss and study a particular issue

constitution: a document that defines and limits the powers of a government and describes how that government is organized

debates: formal discussions where different views are presented

economy: the system by which a country's goods and services are produced, bought, and sold

filibuster: a process involving very long speeches, used to block or delay action on a bill or a vote in the Senate

immigration reform: proposals to change the current laws about how people from other countries can enter and gain the right to live in the United States

impeachment: the formal proceedings in which charges are presented against a public official, with the aim of removing him or her from office

interest groups: groups of people who try to influence government policies, with the aim of advancing their own goals

joint session: a formal meeting of the Senate and the House of Representatives

lobbyists: people who are hired by special interest groups to try to persuade or influence government officials

minimum wage: the lowest wage, set by the government, that companies are allowed to pay their workers

nominates: names to fill an official position or chooses a candidate for office

political parties: groups of people with the same views who work together to win elections

preside: to be in charge of

seniority: having a higher rank, as a result of having served or held a position for a longer time

taxation: the process by which a government raises money from its citizens or residents to pay for the services it provides

term limits: restricting the number of terms an officeholder can serve

United Nations: an international organization formed in 1945 to promote cooperation between countries of the world

veto: a power used by the president to stop a bill from becoming law

vice president: a person who holds the rank just below the president of the United States

*Index

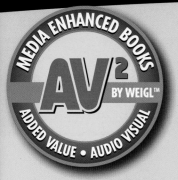

Log on to www.av2books.com

AV² by Weigl brings you media enhanced books that support active learning. Go to www.av2books.com, and enter the special code found on page 2 of this book. You will gain access to enriched and enhanced content that supplements and complements this book. Content includes video, audio, weblinks, quizzes, a slide show, and activities.

AV² Online Navigation

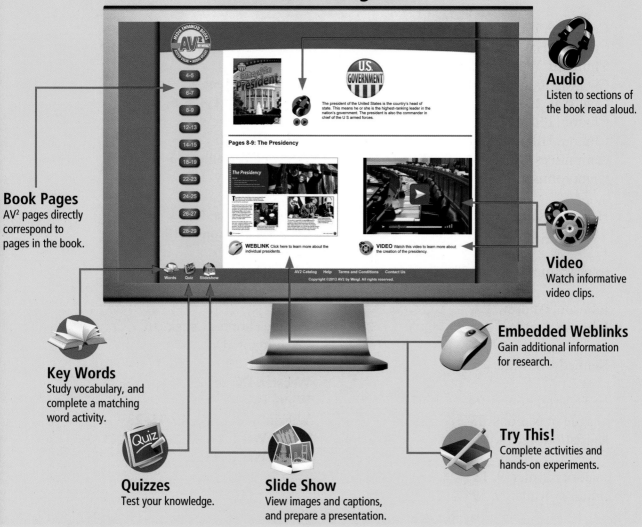

Book Pages
AV² pages directly correspond to pages in the book.

Audio
Listen to sections of the book read aloud.

Video
Watch informative video clips.

Key Words
Study vocabulary, and complete a matching word activity.

Embedded Weblinks
Gain additional information for research.

Try This!
Complete activities and hands-on experiments.

Quizzes
Test your knowledge.

Slide Show
View images and captions, and prepare a presentation.

AV² was built to bridge the gap between print and digital. We encourage you to tell us what you like and what you want to see in the future.

Sign up to be an AV² Ambassador at www.av2books.com/ambassador.

Due to the dynamic nature of the Internet, some of the URLs and activities provided as part of AV² by Weigl may have changed or ceased to exist. AV² by Weigl accepts no responsibility for any such changes. All media enhanced books are regularly monitored to update addresses and sites in a timely manner. Contact AV² by Weigl at 1-866-649-3445 or av2books@weigl.com with any questions, comments, or feedback.